4 HANDS FOR PRAISE

Keyboard Settings for *Piano* and *Synthesizer*

Moderate

Arranged by Teresa Wilhelmi

Lillenas PUBLISHING COMPANY
KANSAS CITY, MO 64141

CONTENTS

A Song of Thanksgiving	8
Guide Me, O Thou Great Jehovah	38
Just as I Am	62
Let Us Break Bread Together	14
Postlude	70
Praise to the Lord, the Almighty	43
Prelude	4
Rejoice, Ye Pure in Heart	27
SWEET LAND OF LIBERTY (Patriotic Medley)	19
America, the Beautiful	
Battle Hymn of the Republic	
Were You There?	50
What Wondrous Love Is This	33

Prelude

TERESA WILHELMI

Moderately flowing ♩ = ca. 86
Synth setting: Jazz Guitar* (General MIDI 26)

*Alternate settings: 12 String Guitar (Expansion sound); Nylon String Guitar (General MIDI 24)

8
8vb
8va
8
12
(8vb)
cresc. poco a poco
12 (8va)
cresc. poco a poco
16
16

19
ff
mp
19
ff
mp
22
22
26
26

29
29
32
Go Back
32
35
rit.
35
rit.

A Song of Thanksgiving

Traditional Welsh Melody
Arranged by Teresa Wilhelmi

Moderate and Cheerful ♩ = ca.102

Synth settings: Bright Piano* (General MIDI 01)
Ensemble Strings* (General MIDI 48)
Piano w/strings (Expansion sounds)

*There are other General MIDI or Expansion settings for Piano and Strings. Use one that you prefer.

8
Strings (GM 48)
Mellow
mp
8
Mellow
mp
12
12
16
𝄋 piano w/strings (Expansion)
rit.
a tempo
16
𝄋 Crisp and clear
rit.
mf
a tempo

20
20
24
Majestic
24
28
28

33
33
2nd time to Coda
37
decresc.
2nd time to Coda
37
decresc.
mp
41
Piano (GM 01)
Spunky
mp
rit.
f
41
rit.
wait for
synth change
f

mp
mp

57
D.S. al Coda
CODA
57
D.S. al Coda
CODA
61
rit.
61
rit.
65
Cheery
a tempo
mp
cresc.
8va
f
65
a tempo
mp
cresc.
f

Let Us Break Bread Together

Afro-American Spiritual
Arranged by Teresa Wilhelmi

Rubato ♩ = ca. 84
Synth setting: Flute* (General MIDI 73)

*If possible use touch vibrato for long notes.

12
Smoothly, in tempo
16
8vb
20
24
Flowing
8vb

28
32
36
mp
mf
39
8va

42
mf
(8va)
mp
45
3
48
52

56
60
8vb
64
68
rit.
decresc.
8va
p
rit.
decresc.
p
8vb

Sweet Land of Liberty

(Patriotic Medley)

Arranged by Teresa Wilhelmi

Briskly ♩ = ca. 92
"America the Beautiful" (Samuel A. Ward)
8
8
11
11
14
14
8vb

17
rit.
mf
a tempo
17
rit.
mf
8vb
a tempo
20
20
24
rit.
a tempo
24
rit.
a tempo
8vb

27
27
31
Faster ♩ = ca. 108
31
35
"Battle Hymn of the Republic" (Traditional)
mf
35
mf

39
39
43
43
46
46

50
50
mp
54
mp
54
58
cresc.
58
cresc.

♩ = ca. 92
62
rit.
f
62
f
8vb
65
65
8vb
Tempo I ♩ = ca. 82
68
rit.
mp
68
rit.
mp
8vb

71
71
75
75
7
78
78
p
p

Rejoice, Ye Pure in Heart

ARTHUR H. MESSITER
Arranged by Teresa Wilhelmi

Majestic ♩ = ca. 92
Synth settings: Church organ* (General MIDI 19)
Slow strings (General MIDI 49)

*Alternate setting: Full pipes (Expansion sounds)

6
6
10
10
13
mf
8vb
13
mf

Slow strings (GM 49)
8vb
8vb
8vb

26
8vb
26
29
8vb
8vb
29
32
32
8va
15ma
cresc.
8va

35
Church organ (GM 19)
f
8vb
35
8va
f
38
8vb
38
41
41

8vb

What Wondrous Love Is This

Traditional
Arranged by Teresa Wilhelmi

Simply with feeling ♩ = ca. 82
Synth setting: Jazz Guitar* (General MIDI 26)

*Alternate setting: 12 String guitar (Expansion sounds)

8
8
12
12
16
16

19
19
Rubato
23
23
26
Tempo I
26

29
mf
29
mf
33
33
37
37

41
decresc.
41
45
mp
45
mp
48
rit.
48

Guide Me, O Thou Great Jehovah

JOHN HUGHES
Arranged by Teresa Wilhelmi

Rubato ♩ = ca.80
Synth settings: Piano with strings
Flute (General MIDI 73)

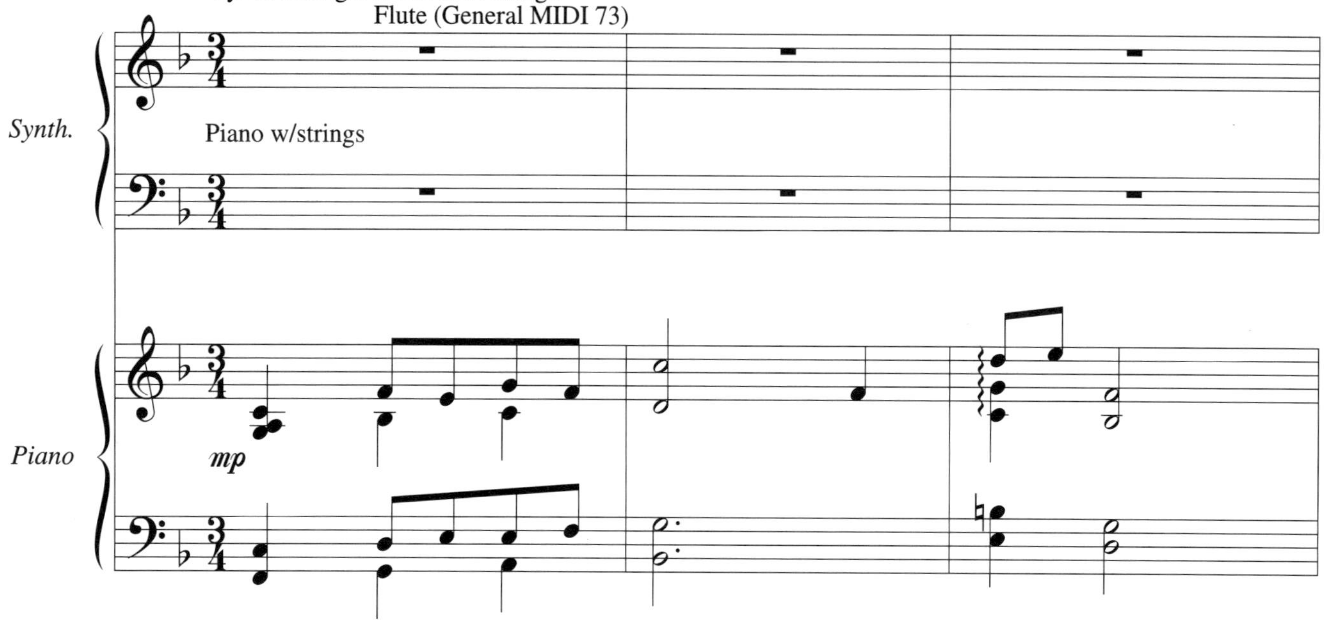

8
rit.
relax tempo
mf
8
8va
rit.
relax tempo
mf
11
11
14
14

f
mp
Cheerfully ♩ = ca.92
Flute (GM 73)

26
26
29
Smoothly
29
33
cresc.
mf
33
cresc.
mf

mp
rit.
mp
rit.
Tempo I ♩ = ca.80
Piano with strings
rit.
rit.
8va

Praise to the Lord, the Almighty

Traditional
Arranged by Teresa Wilhelmi

Cheerfully and solid ♩ = ca. 102
Synth settings: Jazz Guitar* (General MIDI 26)
Church Organ** (General MIDI 19)

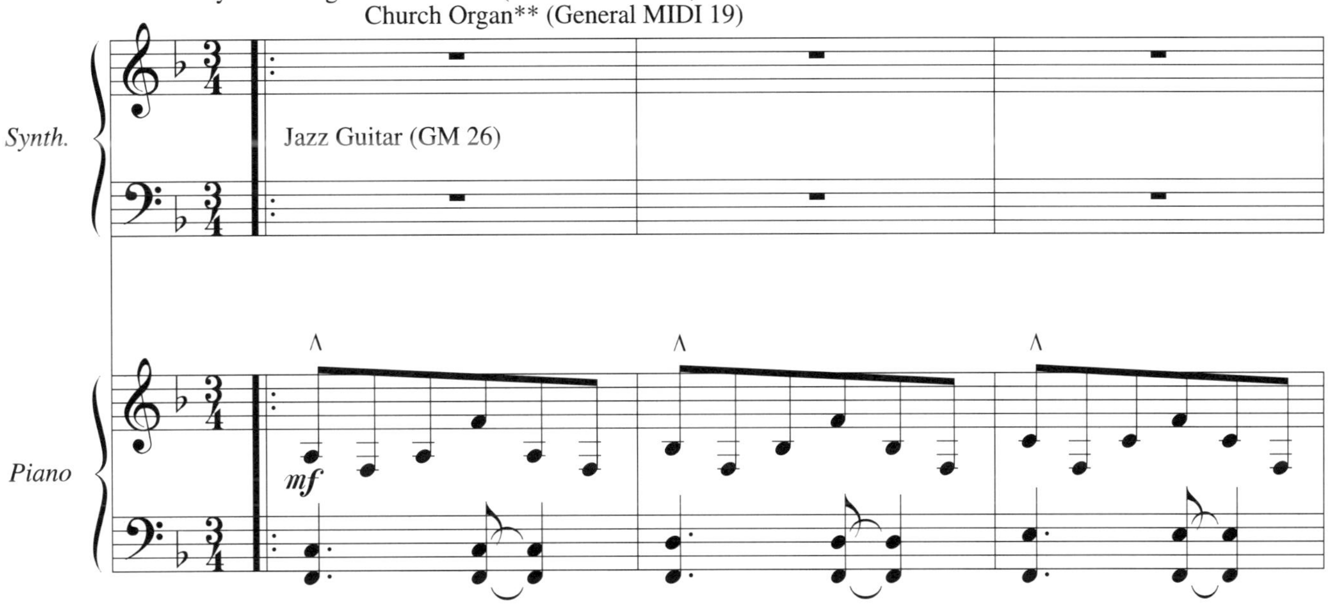

*Alternate settings: Electric Piano (Genereal MIDI 4) - needs to cut through piano part
**Pipe Organ (Expansion sound)

8
mp
8
mp
12
12
16
mf
16
mf
8vb

20
20
23
mp
23
mp
8vb
27
mf
decresc.
gradually slowing
27
mf
decresc.
gradually slowing
8vb

30
30
mp
Deliberate, not too fast
Church Organ (GM 19)
34
ff
8vb
34
ff
37
mf
(8vb)
37
8va
mf

41
8vb
41
8va
Smoothly
44
mp
(8vb)
44
(8va)
mp
48
48

52
cresc.
52
cresc.
Majestic
56
ff
decresc.
56
ff
decresc.
60
mf
decresc.
rit.
60
mf
decresc.
rit.

64
mp
64
mp
67
Faster and very strong
ff
cresc.
8vb
67
ff
cresc.
71
8va
fff
(8vb)
71
fff

Were You There?

Afro-American Spiritual
Arranged by Teresa Wilhelmi

Firm, dark and slow ♩ = ca. 82

Synth setting: Slow strings (General MIDI 49)

10
mp
10
14
14
18
f
18
f

22
22
26
decresc.
mp
26
decresc.
mp
29
Lighter
29

33
33
mf
37
mp
37
mp
41
41
8vb

45
45
49
rit.
49
rit.
slowly accel.
8vb
53
mf
mf
53
mf
mf

57
Deliberate tempo ♩ = ca. 92
57
mf
mp
60
mf
rit.
mp
8vb
Rubato with feeling ♩ = ca. 78
60
mf
rit.
mp
63
63

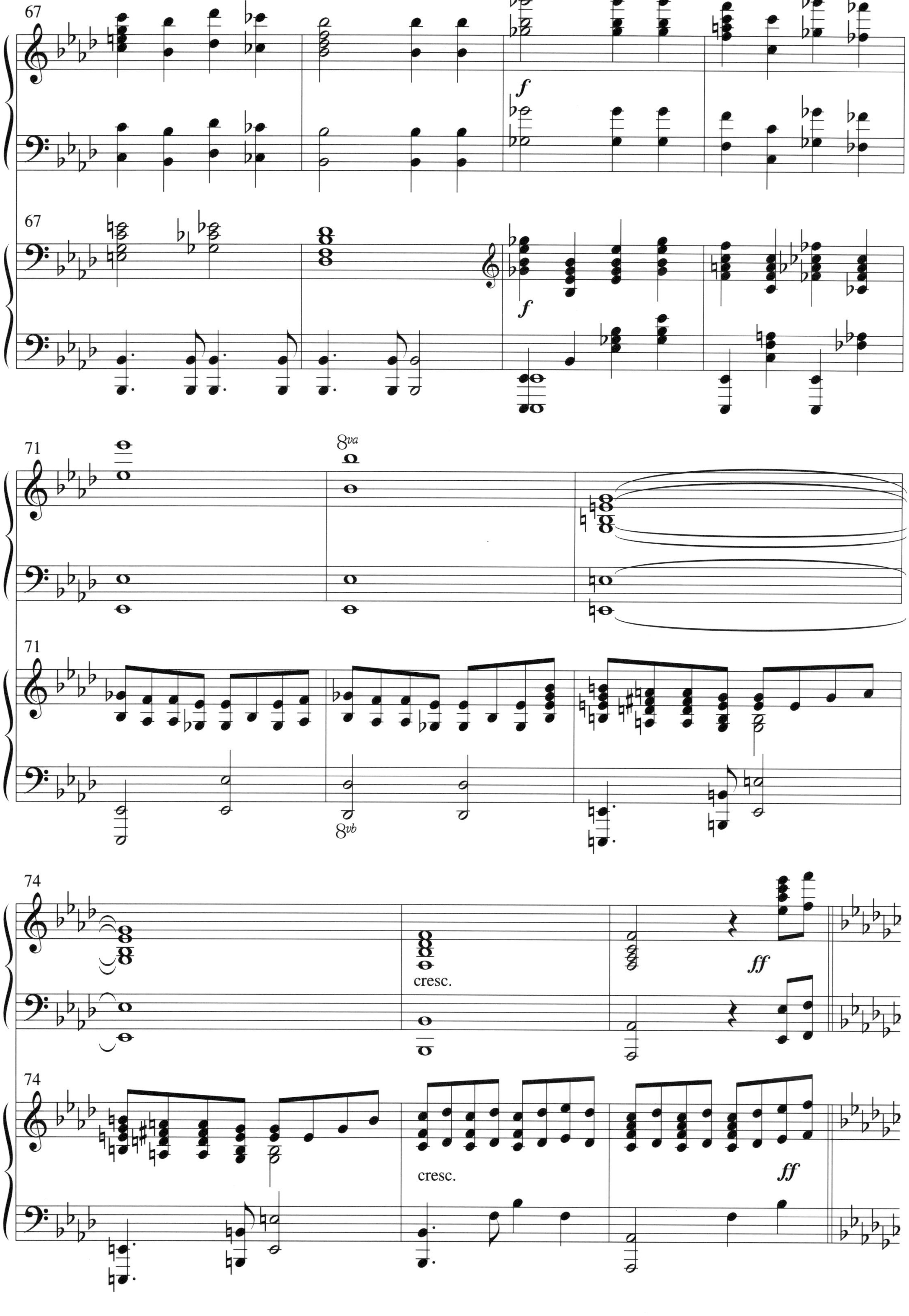
67
f
67
f
71
8va
71
8vb
74
cresc.
ff
74
cresc.
ff

77
sub. mp
77
8va
sub. mp
80
(8va)
80
83
83
mf

Simply, with new feeling ♩ = ca. 82

99
99
103
Triumphantly ♩ = ca. 92
103
8va
mp
cresc. poco a poco
107
8va
8vb
8vb
107
8va
8va
8va

110
(8va)
110
113
(8va)
113
117
Contemplative
mp
mf
mp
117
mp
mf
mp

121
Slowly
ff
121
ff
125
125
128
rit.
8va
128
8vb
rit.

Just as I Am

WILLIAM B. BRADBURY
Arranged by Teresa Wilhelmi

With lots of expression ♩ = ca. 78
Synth settings: Ensemble strings (General MIDI 48)

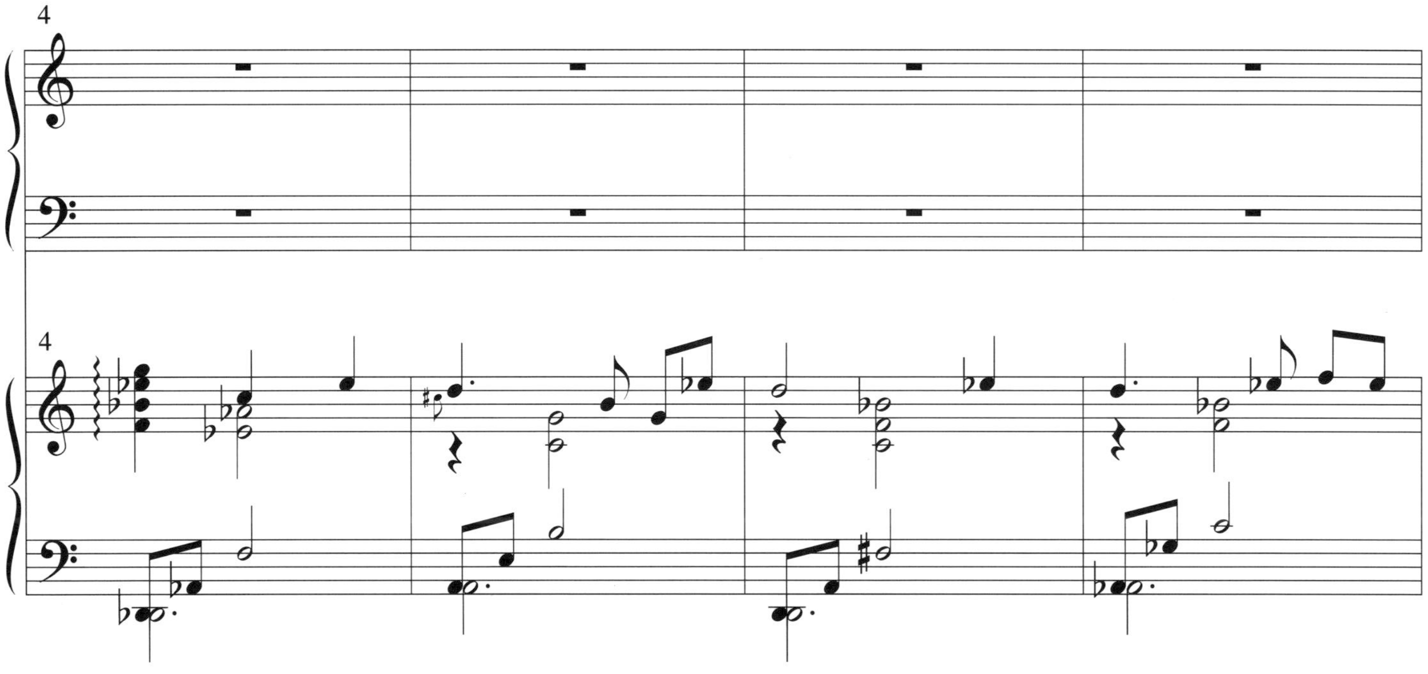

8
mp
8
12
12
16
Stronger
mf
16
mf

20
3
3
20
24
24
27
Not too slow
27

30
30
34
34
37
cresc.
37
cresc.

41
Relax
mf
41
mf
8vb
44
mp
cresc.
44
mp cresc.
48
Grand
f
48
f

52
52
55
55
58
rit.
mf
a tempo
58
rit.
mf
a tempo
8vb

61
61
3
64
64
67
cresc.
5 3 1 3
67
cresc.

71
Expressive
f
mf
71
f
mf
8vb
75
75
79
decresc.
79
decresc.

Postlude

TERESA WILHELMI

Contemplative ♩ = ca. 82

Synth setting: Ensemble Strings (General MIDI 48)

9
(♭)
rit.
a tempo
9
8va
rit.
a tempo
14
14
5 1 2
18
8va
mf
mp
18
mf
mp
8va
8vb